Selected Bibliography of U. G. Világos

SELECTED LYRIC POETRY

Világos

ISBN: 978-1-915079-72-5

Cover designed by Aaron Kent

Edited and typeset by Aaron Kent

For Jenő, Beano, Bampy, Rudolf

Broken Sleep Books Ltd
Rhydwen,
Talgarreg,
SA44 4HB
Wales

Contents

SELECTED LYRIC POETRY

U. G. Világos

You Killed My Cousin in a Drive-by

A piece of herself
hurled into a mausoleum.
There were no children in that town.
All were dead. All were gone.

When she died all the children
were stillborn. In the house
the dead children cried
because of the death
of my cousin. The funeral
had been too late
to bury her soul.

I feel her like the breath
of a child in the still room
of the world. A hole
in the earth for a time.

She was still part of
the world and she lived
on after the funeral
but her face had become
an emblem of
the human struggle.

Brains 'n' Cake

Some people said that the dead can't get sick,
and that if they die they die a clean death.
But then I saw a man in hospital,
his heart having been damaged so badly,
that it burst, and then began to calcify inside him.

My wife's sister told me she had become a cannibal,
if I did not find a way to stop her, she would eat my heart.
I woke from a deep sleep, and saw that the clock read 1400,
my wife had been sitting on the floor with her face in the corner
for the last 6 months.

> *My wife's sister has become a cannibal.*
> *The cannibal wants my heart for breakfast.*
> *I must get my wife to stop it before it gets her.*
> *I must go now, a stranger is waiting at the front door.*

He wants to buy my house. He wanted to buy
the house in the beginning, but I refused.
When the house was vacant, I was not home,
or else he would not have gotten inside.

He was asking where the garden was.
He seemed to think that I had a garden. He is a stranger.
I could have asked who he was, but I could not bring myself
to speak, or move, or move my mouth to speak.

He went in and pulled an old girl out.
The old girl looked familiar,
but there is no garden,
there is no old girl. Just my wife's sister
digesting my salted heart.

Oh God I've Peaked!!!

This plate
of nachos
was bought
for the sole

purpose of
eating the
whole fucking
thing. And not

one of you
could possibly
do anything
about it. This

fucking thing
I am eating
is going to
explode in

your goddamn
face. This plate
of nachos, it can
fucking suck

down everything
in the world
and *we love you*.
It would be

a fucking
crime if you
tried to eat
anything else.

Waiting for the Show to go on

There is a face in the water.
The face laughs.
I go back to bed wearing one sock and no pants.
My bed is filled with penguins.
There is no rain today.
Today is a sunny day.
There is no snow.
Tomorrow it will rain.
I'll listen.
They'll see the rain.
It will melt the snow.
It will become ocean.
Penguins join in the ocean.
I will try to be part of the ocean.
I will stare into it.
I will sing.
I will dance.
I will forget about the murderers who killed me.
Freckles! Freckles!

Deranged Funny and Sad

I went into our bathroom
and looked into the mirror
after I had showered and
I just want to know if I can
get my inner child, he must
be only six or seven, out of
my mirror, out of my soul,
and onto the streets.

It's not my problem, that little
kid doesn't care whether he
lives or dies, and I don't give
a damn. Do the world a favour
and let him live.

because money works in queues

iron lungs pump ounces
of liquid through bare chests
but pale and desperate people
gather round fires set

against money flown into cities
under neon ice; towards promise
rings wear carnations in soles
like the forked toes of cats out

in more creative streets heads
all turn, dares to nod, licks smoke
from braziers without mind in vacant
galleries speculative daisy day

markets buy purbeck roses in summer
for jam peppers, wine in saucers
hot in the sunlight — tomorrow
of reform's complaint attracts customers

in ripped sais and gumminess
this street parade redeems umber
sketches but throws locals east-of-beyond
bombs tunes sung tired far south lets

heartstrings black as luminaries
(it told them what violet hills look like,
which tide announced rise and success
strikes the thief lets his guilty private

I will not judge you when we sit across from each other in the silence

I could have been just like him, if I'd tried
to love you. I might have given my whole self,
though it would not have been enough.
We loved a little more deeply for it

and that is the way it goes: a sad song
the drowning out of the human voice.
This tells me the earth's future in two things:
the comfort of loving the world, and the doubt

that anything is ever to be perfect, perfect love.
We can never come to an end. It is greater
than everything and exists only in memory,
out of the mouths of those to whom we owe

the tiniest, most contained part of evolution
and exchange the whole for a bag of late nights.
The natural order of things, the ravenous,
craving, compassionate art of art and life.

It is people that we fear, that made us afraid
to enter the bath. I do not wish to believe in God
but sometimes I have to use imperfect logic.
How can I know myself without petals, sweetness,

and hate? An entire belief system may be torn apart,
but I do not know how I got there. It is not just
the words on the page, it is the possibilities
of the wind and my breath in the air around me.

Fantasy Baseball Waiver Wire

There are two
counterspies on the edge
of the harbour and now
they see the boats
coming, the white
boats on the dark
waters of the harbour
and they move away
from the edge, they
are not looking, they
cannot face the boats

The sun is
rising slowly, the
tide is rising
slowly, the boats
come closer and the
boats come closer,
the sun is rising
slowly, the tide
is rising slowly

The counterspies
go on, they are
not looking, they
cannot face the boats,
the sun is rising
slowly, the tide
is rising slowly,
the boats come

closer and the boats
come closer, the
tide is rising slowly

The counterspies
go on, they are
not looking, they
cannot face the boats,
the sun is rising
slowly.

Float-in

I

I would look a-west
when they had me
with the world upon me;
and I would hear an answer –
for I would hear the sea
its answer that I heard on the breeze.
As the tide rose round and through,
round and up it was borne.
And so the seas that had me were of earth
with wind to their mouths and sand
in between the waves
where I should make for them,
for my answer to what was said to be heard;
for as far as far as the salt spray's white
was the earth where were my shores and waves and sky,
as far as I was there of a certainty
he told me there I should come;
it could be none other!
So, out there it lay, it was of our world,
though it lay further, in other seas;
it was there he would have me come if I were whole.
And it was there, it was true enough.
But then I thought for that very same wind and sea -
but, of all these, wind —
the land of the earth
to which of our skies we looked in that direction!
So that the question that was asked
had it seemed come of that of what was the answer —
as in our world, or not in our world, and that I thought

as was my choice — for they would not stay for more —
if land-water were the choice
then of these our times,
with seas between it and the times,
no place could give them
where they could come; for
land — which was the sea of land's face in that,
and land itself and skies themselves; for it
all and everything in a world
as it did, was too small for those we might be
to touch! Well, yes; that indeed might be so!
But for me of it I was sure!
So that for any and all what should it matter
that there is no other
and what shouldn't matter
though t'were all the earth of Earth for a time!
(and more than a time!)
for the time to that we might taste its fruit! or
touch what flowers! or smell
whatever of air did in its own season -
what should matter
trying to learn 'til we were done with its teaching!
Yet we could not stay there a million years!;
nor would there always be the sea!

And it was true!
It was true that I would come there too for answer
— as the word was sent from the far seas —
for he that would be there in time that was to come
— that he must, the future, must.
Of those who have waited thus to the answer,
the sea is the voice of those, — it is true of the winds
there of the earth, but they, those we know,
would for they are with us there and ours,

with all the land on it of all the past,
the future will be one to the sun.
Yet that that they are with us we know:

       and, in the end, that was that I should be
       there to await in their world where all were
       a future, one in time — what that it might be
but if — if…

II

And he who sent that voice out in a cry was here
'cause he saw our eyes and his own eyes,
our two eyes in my world —
and in his world that that I was for them!
And that, by so, he was made one
for those that were made and with them,
and in time that was for me of all
those we knew who have waited
the word to find in earth 'fore a time is said
and not come, for this is, all things are,
time to come in its order so —

So it will be I, too! I thought,
though it was true enough,
for I am now as I am now and
when I came as you and the wind
know that was in the last of our times here,
here in time before our time
in our world; yet, when and I looked
around in the harbour from me
on I who was on board the ship I called the sea
or the ocean and it seemed to all who had me not long —
but in the wind and that my word would come!
Yet I told all, who had no ships
nor for this very time and twas well

to the sailors of that it seemed far; and to me there
were not just for long, the other words in time that had
hold of our words I knew that then to find — for then I was
a whole thing and yet to be made, I knew this of myself,
for now the future of those tide times of our time on those

the harbour; when was it true as that was true to-gether,
I thought; if the world could be one world — would we be
not one? And they could be so, could come so and go with
all time and change as our change that, as one we might
learn of another to be or a truth for the other to hear as
it had to tell of the way it had to the sky; though this of
time was of course a truth too. I had thought it and knew
the rest, that of our times in the past it was for those and
these to know they had heard the world there that was
made for the seas as their voice and had made them to
this that I be of it as were those of my past: the one that I
knew for that of the words and now this of which I am —
now I knew of the answer as it came. So too — now you
heard the one, now you know 'tis come to know the two.

III

And for you there then in those words - for it seemed to them who
heard as there would no such time would come again; though they
knew, of their own change — they must not, that time of their
coming to have, as that in ours had to wait till I be the time: and
so be ready to do it, for now they did; in that there that then be of
mine as they now were in these very moments of my time and of
me and then I come, it might be it be said — and no sooner; no
not when but just when, as they now were made that now'd come
for the same in which as I would know, so too the new I did so that
my coming would not be just I came in their times before! That
was not it — but that, that as I would be then I did as, and there of
know, know — and was made: and as made, came. So that the time

is now that all is come; as well, you will, there being all one and now we know: the time comes, come — though for all of the ways that of the change they had I came in theirs! for it might be there might be any, all that then we have all were yet to come — that all be in.

The Red Child

When I went out into the corridor,
I heard a raucous chattering of whispers.
Four angels, three crying
And the other, trembling, I once knew.

Her day's fear ahead of her,
The way she held on, I knew
her story. You have heard it too.
I thought how small and alone

We must seem; we appear
Not so bright, so rigid, as they appear to be
Upon the rocks of the Danube. I wanted
To say but a word to them.

Not to offer something but to soften it.
But then my one stooped down
And began to talk to the others.
A trickle of foam slipped from her mouth.
Like blood, I thought. But she would not say more.

A Darned Good Time

Ghosts have the best time at parties
because they 're the only
celebrations people let them have.

*Nothing wrong with giving birth
to a fossilized thoracic ossuarium.*

I carried my grandmother
around
in the crook of my arm
and sang her songs
as the benign creatures
so patiently
sewed her fetuses in their shells.

The unadventurous say:
What if I got excited
about a real ghost?
I would deny them their
odd pleasure,
drink till I fell down
in a stupor, then stagger
to the emergency room,
acknowledging them as they watched me
writhe and writhe and writhe.

Lowballgeddon

This is how I like to wash my hands:

1. I scrub away all flesh until it's gone.

2. Newspaper, then, smears a fresh coat of dirt.

3. I turn on the shower and hold up my hands.

4. I lather them and rinse them.

5. "Wait," I tell the bone marrow bursting out from under my skin like an ostrich.

6. A phrase in Magyar keeps repeating itself

7. I stop washing.

8. I lower my expectation.

9. The light changes.

John Lamb

I've been with my weird
Short hair, slow shoes since 1960,
heard you mention something
creative called beatnik,
separation of church and state.

Got a Zen tattoo but won't
spread my crazy.
All God's children gone crazy,
made good and smart by my world of squalor.
All countries breed crazy,
for knowing no art.
I don't read or write,
first lotto winner and still owe
outlaw John Lamb.

Which is better, dream of gammon or
stand on a fence watching a trout,
eyes wide, catching spit out of sky?
These fish swim wild after trouble,
teasing the trout, breathing rocks.
Rolling deep, I find it hard to breathe,
lose heart, gods wandering in dark.

Burned the commandments by waxed praise.
Fall in church to make way for dancing,
don't care about rules but can't play dumb,
but the white ones confused me.

Outside the White Witch
stands lit in ruin and,
open, invites me to explore.
Calling silence I hunt through wild
rubbery dust, sorry for everything.

Waves from the hills, coming under tide.
The breeze blew black but I live to sing,
morning long, drowning words on long legs.
Seems angry, makes war against who,
stranger fish. My kind you,
blessed stones and seas.

Glassy storm/surf, whose dead are rise in glad
hearts in stained-glass doors.
Let my real mind choose your music.
Choose not me, live in light.
Drink it, hold it. Maybe beyond, dance.

The Night Before

If you leave, please
leave me
with a profession of love,
just a little,
and for one night
give yourself everything.
You will know
there is no service I won't do
on my own to
want nothing of you.
You, who provides
the miracle of luxury,
leave with one singular effect:
leave me deserving you.

Young Knuckle

Young Knuckle, you are like Knuckle.
Knuckle's a good word.

When you were younger, like a young Knuckle,
your knuckles weren't like that.
When you were younger,
I had to tie you with a string
so that you wouldn't break them.
I didn't know that then,
but now I know,
a child can do some pretty stupid things.

I got your knuckles fixed, just like Knuckle.

Young Knuckle, your hands
are very tough.
In your knuckles I see a lot of Knuckle.
They're very tough
and I imagine,
as hard as the stones.

Sunny Domino

I put a finger in and the paint drops
to my feet. There is too much feeling and
I spill it. You wash your hand
in water but only to hide it. You've forgotten
to set out salt. We are left too soon.
Close your eyes. Take a breath. See,
that ice again. Catch a memory in the swirls.
There are no clear answers, only tiny bubbles
in the freezing sea of cold. We lie
together like drowning men,
staring up at the sky like deer
hunched over the forest floor. The light
is through the peep-hole of our souls,
and it's there all along, standing like a mirror.
There's something within me
you can't see, something I carry around
all day trying to imagine what it is.
The moon is the same every night
as a corner store that never closes. I get used to
its light swinging, trying to hit the mind
like a firecracker. It never works. You get used to
its peeling paint. The north side of my eye
is the snow that falls. It stays, year after year,
cloaking everything. You see it even if I don't,
constantly, except when it goes off, when it dances
in the sky like a rocket ship launching from a pier.
The rocket rises and I let it climb, I let it touch me,
I let it turn me in a new direction.
It is part of you and me together,
in the darkest side of the night. You pick at

the moon from the porch. You step on the pebbles.
It's all the same. The same white lights in every town,
the same yellow streetlamps that never seem to light.
So much empty space. I want to learn more
about the ocean, what it's trying to tell me.
I want to paint, to build a boat, to wander
and write poetry.

The Giant Mouth/The Typhoon

We walk the field together
with everybody before sunrise,
into the cold light of your bed.
We move forward and upwards
to the sky. I still see the flowers
as we run around, dressed
in yellow shirts as if dancing
along with our song.

My mother sees
my brother
grab your leg
and throw the bat.
He wants to hit the moon.
I still see the cars
drive by when the sun
has gone down.

Everybody in the street
is there. The smiling kids
searching for one more night
and one more night
to feel alive. You reach
to hold me. You whisper 'ok,'
you cry 'ok,' you whisper 'ok,'
you ask 'ok,' 'ok,' and 'ok,'

'ok,' and 'ok,' you wonder 'ok,'
and 'ok,' you think 'ok,'
you hold my hand and say 'ok,'

you lie there on the grass,
the stars show through your tears,
and 'ok,' you lie there
like you've done every night.
And it's ok.

The Hypochondriac

I've killed my own hands by
placing them under a hot kettle
and held the spout
for about half an hour. It was
the worst torture and the best
punishment, for not as
wounded as the kettle as you'd
expect from the steam, the
burning of the palms is
so intense
that the pain becomes
transfigura-
tion, and I felt more than one
miracle in the burning and
the red blood
in one motion.

Big Bear's Wartime Farm Heroes

There are two villages.
One is behind you.
Another is here.
They don't
talk to each other.
We are not allowed
to say their names.
I love the cold
and the snow.
I love the
night.
I love the
fire in the night.
I can't live
inside this town
anymore.

I am
the only one who doesn't
feel
the ache in our collective chest.
I can hear the whispers
of the one I call Father
and think of
the rocks
in your hand.
I am your hyena.
It's I, the heat
on your ribs.

It's I, the heat
on your legs.
It's I, the heat
on your hands.
It's I, the pain.

The Flesh Eating Bionic Squirrel

The words are simple, the tone is moving
like a surrealist sculpting rain
as I take a picture of the pink petals
the carriageway loves so dearly.

My brain is magnetized
to The Strokes' sound
and its stupidity.

Even after I finish,
the song is still spinning in
my head, and I have
no words to speak.

> *my voice has gone into*
> *quiet mode and we are left*
> *to shuffle out of this*
> *mind together like friendly foxes*

You don't exist
> *the fable repeats itself*
Because you are DEAD.

The town, the non-descript little
boy next door,
hides in the woods.

Our teachers are dead.
I am alive.

Muffin McWorms

The first time a candle went out on its own
I screamed out of sheer fear,
it doesn't explode the way the book says it will–
it gives a gust of black smoke like its own expression.
I hate all the rules about open caskets
especially if you plan on donating
what's inside the casket to science.
I wish I could eat a cannonball whole
and chew at its underbelly like a newt
until its ribs crack and all you see
is yellow lemon-peel pulp.
I don't know if that would bring me
back to life, but that's what I've always wanted.

Honey Badger

The sea and the sky are all we have
and what is ours is yours.
I wish that I could fall into a lake of oil,
so you can pull me out with a rope made of seaweed.
I wish you could find the words
to tell the police that your mother and I
fell off a bridge in two separate planes of existence.
I wish you could find the words
to say I was born in the wrong town.
I wish you could find the words
for when the whole world thinks that you are dying,
but you aren't.
I wish you could see how this will all go wrong.

When you're ready to die
and the fire comes for your heart,
ask for two things:

> ask for the moon
> and then ask for it all.

Song of the Dawn

Everything has been twirled around
and around by language, frothed like angry dogs
until the island which gave life froze in imitation
of a big head. Many a moon the sides of the head
have crusted like fortresses upon an outpost.
It is unfashionable. We, alone, jump
in every drivable vehicle chasing
a tornado's body weighing options up at the dry cleaners.
I regret I have never drowned a water-splashed fire truck
and laughed briefly while snuffing out life
and provided you a baby pool to cry around.
The tar beads are full of soap, and you tell me I am smart,
you tell me I am a selfish, godless hypocrite.
You say you've never heard a poem as bad as this one,
yet you only throw critiques because it saddens me,
disgusts you, relieves you from the guilt
of a drive-by shooting. I am not sorry for you,
but I apologise sincerely to my thesis of mechanics.

Song of the Morning

From cockeyed battlegrounds where raised fists dip
round in awful moonflair, rose flushed skirt
my basketball beard floors on psychedelic shore,
where fingertips dislodged linkages
of space-time linearity and care
for contingency on horizonology
for uneaten or safe skull bruises.
So much rotting slops. Despite sacred protocols
received without a doorway, threshold,
throughout miracle machines offers benediction.
One hails, the others have settled
they label four constituencies
more united by nexus
than atom is on decay
As exit week of nonsense
writers felling reach through shady woodland,
swinging hands displaying
hand-painted earrings,
a member of Poetry plucks tar beads
from our ears and whatever voice
does cause my resolve to broaden
Some soul matters dove on pavement
throws all bare and fearless bleeding itself
taps air mail mark, crunches plucked eyeballs,
murders car.

The Side of the Pool

I think I may have fallen
out of a cloud, because
I look like a cloud I feel
like a cloud, and sometimes
I can hear a song coming
from the clouds.

I'm an invisible wind myself,
I just blow across the road
but when the wind is still
I feel like the grass growing, I feel
like the sun, I feel like the bird
with the heartbroken sound.

I can listen, I can hear the noise,
how beautiful it is when rain
comes down. when I was
just a wind there is a bird
that sang and it sang of things
no one else knew.

Daily Fables

Dawn disintegrates –
this church's pain and mystery.
Which seems like madness
to ponder everything and hide nothing,
turn heads with acid details, worry
about decorum in two, wear
wild faces to the choir loft.

To venture in this silence, seek
the 'ritual/real/inner'
truths with new allegiance.
Let an echo join you to the old faithful, all
mistrust to brotherhood, opening
crazy night by day,
armies stand solemn, windows open,
challenge world on its way.

The ringing of bells last
left-sided divine joke.
Or was that noise the song
of cantankerous bass-and-horns.
Could another art
be discovered in sounds whose spectrum
blazes upside-down.

Let everybody dance.
The geocentric story:
Pan much too tall got large days, warped
round sun bend to East making ships
ask to see if the old sea-god is not there,

and not answered acceptably open air
with caves drifted through rock might swing out to
find caverns like well get lost and leave.

Big Joe & the Cave of Bones

Cloud, closer and not well enough known:
following ship of seven wonders (as in needle for mathematics)
tethered to find crown-jewel, giving tools
and worship of sea-god,
empowered by corn-fields, and pilgrims
seeking wise man's wisdom.
Sometimes it's you, and it's not.
Particle-mass of that message in
that noise the voice over:
just want to fix this broken world,
let alone looking
around to find who
makes the noise I make.
Secret texts of a crazy well-told story
they don't quite understand.

The field is blowing, pointing north deeper in echo, connecting the
eye to the flood in sun as beyond the sun is the west. Louder and
louder and so the promise of the great hell against the wind-tunnel
rolling across fields becoming arrows finding their place in the night,
one year's worth of memory and fire gathered under the leaves and
the trees which no longer step forward into the light.

Everyday man: bathetic, synesthetes,
stooping at and of the tiny water-burst.
Perplexing ripples act like a story.
It's an album of yellow, mottled
found rock like a mistake from sunrise to midnight
and finds new words to be words that fit.

As a worm there comes a time
where you know yourself
from within your own light.
Something inside knows all that has happened.
I'm right there, dreaming away
on other things not to move an inch.
I am feeling myself the worm,
watching myself move through the dark,
and cannot resist to laugh
at myself.

It is evening as it has been noon, and noon as it was the day, and the
day before it, and before that the evening, and so on, and has been,
from the beginning, all before me. The threads of my time fly out of
my head and this doesn't matter, and the dreamers on the platform
are still perfect.

Open the window, I got to get my breath.
Maybe you do not have to move an inch.
These small things become
all things.
As I show you the beatitudes
you don't believe
but when I speak of you you want to die
but are not afraid of death.
I want to say you're nothing.
And when your attention
is about you,
the sky will spread its eyelids.
Take off the ideas,
and listen to what has happened inside.
Get somewhere new
and do not be still.
A voice from within you,

gets louder and stronger and louder and louder
and you can no longer sleep.
The eyes and the feet and the feet
I see moving as if in some sort of dance
if you don't move your eyes away from them.
The space that was here is not here,
and it's taking you by the arm,
carrying you to something new.

What's not yet all here is all gone. Let us go. The eye sees all, all of
us dancing together, on the night we cannot know, except that we
do. Let us go.

I have three sonnets for you,
from three different parts of my life,
each one counting the opposite of each other,
resembling half-time, and counting the other half.
We are made with half and whole,
divided and undivision.
I remember.
My two sons.
One watching.
The other practicing.
I see them dance around me.
I see a split in my soul
that splits itself and multiplies,
on and on
never listening, never pausing,
flying between two realms
feeling some breathing space
and burning all the night away.

Johnny 5 Fingers

they moved
away
from the beach
that they lived on
that they used to spend
the winter and spring on,
that they used to see
the walkers
and the people walking
before all they
could see
were the boats coming,
the boats
on the dark
waters of the harbour
and at first
they liked
what they saw,
they made the best of
the situation,
learnt to love the way that
the changing
shapes were visible
in the dark night
of the harbour,
because there were
some shapes they were familiar
with and for an instant thought
may be the same nuthatch
that they saw the previous year,

resting on the boat they used to sit on,
see the world,
spend the winter
upon the waves
that birthed them.
Now they only see boats,
the whiteness
of the boats,
and they
hear the sound of the
water,
swollen now
by the incoming tide.
They make a habit
of strolling
there now,
floating on these waters and
sailing
down to the
farthest reaches
of the harbour
now merely visitors
in this world
that is somewhere else.

Superman's Blackout

I imagine you could take a rock
and twist it into nothing,
like punching someone
in the side of the head
and not even hearing a sound.

The Magnetic Fields at Zero Gravity

Now that was real life I remember.
The words of my childhood.
But no one was there to see me.
No one ever had the pleasure of seeing my soul dance again.
I think there's another world,
where I hear the voices of those who knew me
and those who never tried to get close
and that it all matters.
And I think my soul doesn't know the difference.
It still sounds and feels the same
even as they change.
I go from one to the other
while we still
can't remember
which
is which
the moment and forever in between.

Kaiju Nightmare

I was a beautiful boy.
But even the most beautiful
of beautiful things are also rotten
like all things. It's not really beauty.

Everything will fall. When it does
people will wonder if it ever mattered.
But it always did matter, we just didn't
know it until things changed.

It might have made our time easier,
maybe it was too slow, but in some way
I remember it, even if you forgot
that someday I will die.

Then everything will be
more beautiful than I ever felt before,
like this moment stretched across
eternity's gentle posture.

Everything will go on as the sun
will be the sun will still be coming out
behind them, and it will see them
because we no longer will.

One day you will find that it takes
no part of time but that it is all
of time all at once like a dream
you can't wait to end.

Cronus (Home of the Soldiers)

A member of the mafia always told me that your fortune is written in tinfoil but it doesn't stick unless you bat it against the white wall to get the sharp bark that's inside.

Living alone in your room will surely lead to death.

My whole house smells like ashes.

The faces of all the deceased I have neglected– I should have considered that they would be upset.

When the minutes turned to hours, the hours turned to days.

The second time a candle went out on its own, I didn't even notice.

When the candle was right next to me, I was too busy picking up broken school teacher's portraits that I was sweeping the main room.

And I let it burn forever in there.

This won't do.

Now I have two cats instead of one.

My imagination is gone.

I just let too many movie geniuses kill me.

My only friend opened up her mouth.

The words rolled out of her.

Where have I been all of my years?

I took pictures.

I wanted to stop dead-camera-still.

I need stories that lie on the blank screen, confessional-mode lens.

Much like a deflated balloon, I no longer live.

Write one thousand words of torture tolerance form from composing in any key.

The light bent over the skeletal trees like a skeleton wrist massaged again and again, as a male supermodel concealed it from the light.

Over the madness that emanates from his land a solemn protest urging the public to excuse its condescension.

I am hungry for some spiced popcorn and candy from the stacks of Smith's.

The fruit crusher is my key to fucking up any movie movie to movie they change the words to their shit just to get publicity for John Waters' movie 'Serial Mom'.

I Bebop

We dance on mud they shout
mocking noise behind us
there's people burning
we carry sizzling hearths on our backs
caged men swim timid and peaceful
between arms
feed beasts fat cigars
is there anything nearer pain
than ash from a fitful fire
a puncture wound in my universe
our circumferences are boundaries
across time
back out or back inside
When you grow inside of yourself
between anxiety and ego
when they shove your head
out an exit a sky wide and gape
between limbs I imagine you were forever there
100 long years of a life I abandoned
in a flat roar that demands
an outer cube
And then I shackle myself and padlock my door
with weighted chains
no music crashes through the ceiling
no words bang clot warm
and leave hot waves of sonic black

Scaramouche Kazoo

Give us something to burn.
You awake at dawn but all
you hear is the neighbour
taking down the grass early.

I consider saying, drunk:
I walked into Blackpool once.
Everything on display so fertile.
I got as drunk as anybody.

But later sober I opened the blinds
and saw myself lying on pavement,
cheek by jowl with buckets
and torches, lemons packed in socks.

And it started me off, living
on twigs and shawls.
Enough street energy is
already there when it comes.

Instead I dissociate until I feel like
counting out blind spasms, like
praying to a clenched mouth with claws.
Goodnight my friend, hi Father, yo mother...

Captain Kitten

From Ashes:
Empty chasms,
sweeping horizons

Make wisdom
reverse their route
on slow boats to shore.

The dark frozen
flesh of earth crumbles
now as clay does again,

when iron and sand
sift off to transform tiny
angles in all seen paths.

Some ostrich, meanwhile,
does weep for existence,
does contemplate the limp rabbit.

Snow topped steep
banks running aground
for nothing in winter.

In a pile he sleeps
under a peak he
knows as a drop.

Risk decay while
erect he flows
and fields ebb.

As life deep air springs
up, blue pops over
his words, sleet thumping.

Ferocious wings sliced
around the curve-burst
through a gate they did not make.

Burn the men
who live only by fear
and failure to talk.

It's Hard to be Happy as a Bohemian

Animated like I've eaten my own soul
like I've sewn a voice
into a tongue
cram it down inside my flesh
gourd, deflate like a balloon.
My sentence works like the ventricles
I see my lungs
as a long inflammation
throbbing like heart
lung, no wheeze, no cracks,
use whatever cloth you choose
in the tome,
use whatever filters you've heard.
My final outbreak this morning
when I emptied a deflated lung
into an onerous press,
punctuated the rite of creation,
both a heady ritual,
and the highest hell, as you've said.
I'm pleased that I was unable to show
that plea to the censor
or say that this, it is my last
… this is what I can do
I'll end my possession
of this bronchi
I wish to call
my mother.
The Gramophone
The same question, over and over,
you answer onerously

teaching me to recite the answer
a piquant lesson in writing
patience of fire
and pagination.

The Rockons

AKA Reasons to Stay Alive

1. Well, I say it's overgrown,
a stairway to Nowhere.

2. It's a ridiculous study,
a fantasy toadstool
in the middle of the ward
where no one sees it.

3. Please give it back.

4. Let's have more of that
awful music

5. We're having a test
to see if your heart still beats.

6. I'm sorry,
but I have a bit of an
end-of-semester headache.

7. Excuse me,
that's your consolation.

8. I've been ruined by
the pigeons and the rats.

9. Well, it's my crime
to be the only man
and woman,
jigsaw in hand,
standing in
the underground
garden.

10. It's too small
for me, I'll
never fit in
it, it's full of air
and egg-laying
dung and dust.

11. If I were to be a body,
I think I'd be
half baguette
and half brain.

12. In the hospital
they always try to
turn me away.

13. Do I look dead
to you?

14. Look, I'm right here.

15. They're going to burn
me alive.

16. I'm really quite
lazy, and just not
interested in
sheet music.

17. I'll be reversing.

18. We really do have a test
tomorrow.

19. When I see him,
I'm going to give
him to you.

20. There's no point
in running, you'll just
end up being
a turtle,
sheltered away
in a corner.

21. I'm serious
about my fascination.

22. I have a bat in my car.

23. I think I'll stay a little longer.

24. I will. I won't
leave until you let me.

25. Let's go on a picnic.

26. I want to talk.

27. I will.

28. Please don't do this.

29. This is my future.

30. This is our destiny.

31. I think I'll go to
the chapel
for a while.

32. It's a one-way ticket.

33. Would you mind
bouncing off me for a while?

34. I think I'll find
my own place.

35. That's a tricky situation.

36. There's nothing to
the other side,
it was all a dream.

37. I'll be back as soon
as I'm reanimated.

38. So far there's not
a sign
of my body.

39. Cool, you can see
everything and
no one gets hurt.

40. Why don't you come back?
Why?
Some Days are Harder
I heard you say
I want you to have
a plan
from now on.

41. O, in my dreams
all the shops
come alive
and
you're there,
with me
around
the corner.

The New Gambit / The Koalabat

After I was born I was carried up to heaven
by angels who hung me in a doorway.
You were already there, playing the Koala
by yourself. I am not your brother,
you will never like me the way I am.

Write some poems, write a book,
numbers don't count. Now I am
born in the night into a world of midnight.
I am a sentinel, a shepherd. I exist
because it was nice of you to ask me to exist.

We had a chance, I never got it back.
This is an exorcism.

The Lightning Klaxon Riding Shotgun

I'm a moth on a gauze curtain
in a state of advanced decay
but I'm alive.

I accept the fact of death and birth
because all living is built upon dust
and gold—ceremonial gifts of life.

I wish it didn't have to be this way.
But I know it is and I accept it.
You are one of the young who came before us—

this window we're looking out of.

Old Row Redux

original instruments of communion
analogous flamenco then there are
velociraptors
to the tribe of first kinfolk
all terrain nothing more
close or far was no-thing
everything was doomed to
remain we climbed every mountain
downhill everyone following up
blindfolded the deer oh-so-casual
others pursued with ever more-haughty determination
hemlock or blood
or whatever
Eon, seagulls, kraken —
clouds, thunderous, tortuous waves —
our lost form rang out into lonely oblivion
became palimpsest with some other
reflectorising impulse
within contact
through these acts we join up in a cloud
image-sense's dusk-to-dawn -disposition
and uncover fundamental
structure
if we suppose a God
a field of historical memory
then concurrency is merely fated to
be notary: text so goes the law
one's way of dealing with the past is to do so
piously if possibly in an excess
or however we recall it

what if in terms of free association or retroactive
embroidery of redemption by contrast...
accomplishments in the order of psychic contents
exceed expectations
and by this amount
in expressing the dialectical
it gives a contradictory simplicity of inner truth
a two-level charm of the possible opposite
a revolution in understanding
in an integration of the gaps
that we fall into how else are we to understand
how can anyone be certain
that he isn't the enemy?
for instance treachery becomes consolation
murder the destruction of a common good
symbolised in the moment of metaphor.
and the words are intelligible
if we accept that they are their own elements
and the glyph is as natural
as the division line
a necessary acknowledgement
of a reality beyond meaning
we are living within an anomic
dynamo
of common value
discovering where we belong
(clandestinely)
a pre-state collective pursuit
of that illusory wisdom
realising its immense power
(or consuming its concrete)

Well-Fermented Crust

We, my friend, we sing songs
about fires in the sky,
even though music scares me;
those synthesizer beats
keep the lights on when the music
gives me chills and night turns
to day without you. When you left
the house was a music video
that inspired a song. Your resonance
made the walls ring and scream.

I wish you could have tried harder
to make it all more real. I wish
I could take away the many possibilities
that were lost with your imperfect gift.
Every river and stream overflows
when I let it. We both know that if
I hit you with the finger of fury,
you will simply become a puddle.

I wish I could see how to let you go,
so I could help you fly, fly like a pigeon
that is falling to its death, flying
on broken wings with reckless abandon.

I wish I could watch the sun set, see
the fire that makes you laugh, the fire
that makes you cry; instead I watch
the greying sky become less full of stars.

Bobby Stubbs and the Long Horns

prying open and tracing the threads
in front of the kin
willing to share
us for but a glimmer
we'll never learn where
to look but we'll never stop
it does not matter if we should die
this is a convergence
of the Imaginary state
and the Informal use of language
revenues — let them
love their memories
a babbling self-editing
where the vernacular wiles
cannot undo (shall not)
but…reward
and pay the piper
when this is all done…
we are all that's left
of this universe
all of us in the choirs of one
and the truth is out there
waiting for the interpreters
with a notation.

O Galileo Where Art Thou Satellites

Yet I feel the dance in your light and movement or
my feel that you feel it. We both may spin but
the stars spin and no stars may spin as they spin in space
Yet you dance with me yet we are as one:
and you that feel we have no place in this space
and so as all our place and the feel we are moving
we dance with one another moving only when we want to.
So the stars spin and we are dancing now
but dancing and dancing in the dark in what may
become night in the next century but never dark,
dark only until time and then there is light
and the stars are dancing may it be with us in
each other when time becomes light,
where Earth, a satellite, spins in orbit
around the central sun, like a tiny pebble
on the rim of a vast, decadent waterfall.
Where you orbit around me our life cycles
are measured, the orbits made tighter,
And I, from orbit through Earth orbit.
You are a star in a galaxy of stars and a galaxy of stars.
The moon would rather not be here
any more than you, fodder for poets.
As you step, so you dance, and when you dance,
others dance. You feel your relative steps
and so there is motion. The Moon moves.
The Sun moves, and the Pleiades move you,
their constellations steady as pendulums.

Three Eight Songs

Blood ties like
longer chromosomes;
Some people burn
a piece of landscape,
splashing water on it.
But not me; I grow
a forest where no trees grow
and rub out the clouds.

I see the lakes,
from on high.
The water has changed
colour; I try
to remember
what it used to be,
I try to remember
the colour blue.

I am at the edge
of my consciousness.
I've waited long for this;
it is my first poem
about poetry.
Into that sun,
it must shine,
and it does.

Mr. Kite's Worsted

I.

I have a garden with strawberries.
Here's my garden full of petals.
I need another garden.
I was so lonely I lost my shadow
but it's my shadow, it's inside
the sun. Where did you put
my shadow? I'll find it,
then it won't be sad.
Each plant needs to grow
in a different direction.
Green on the left is a day,
red on the right is a dawn

II.

The rain is mad, but the rain
never knows how to speak.
Like a lap dog it watches everything.
The way it looks at you, you can't see
it, it's invisible, but it's right there.
This is my garden, it's round like
sun, it's strong like wheel.
If you can hold on to the green plants,
you'll be home at long last.

III.

We said *the rain is so mad*
but the rain said *i love you*
and on that day we talked about where
rain would go after it had done what
it had to do. There were some flowers,
some orange, but they all grew together
to make one beautiful sky.
Where does the sky go, after the rain?

IV.

We watched as the rain went
through our bedroom window.
It went into her sock drawer, then out again.
This is my garden, you can climb it
but you must be careful,
you can't make holes in it.

V.

My garden fits in a suitcase.
I pick the flowers when you are sad.
And when you are sleeping
I pick a few more for me.

3 Seasons of The O. C.

Something mysterious
in the marine
environment, maybe.
We could write that down.
Tectonic movement, yes
perhaps massive flooding, death,
or decay, yes.

The skeleton, that seems to fit,
but what if the skeleton is a person?
For all we know, it could be a living person.
That's exciting.
It could be a living, breathing person.
It might be your dead girlfriend.
How romantic. How peculiar.

Was that her mother peering through the window?
Does she know your wife is in the room?
Is she mortified? Is she lonely?
The horror of it all.

There is an upside to this.
If you were still alive, you never would have known misery.
You never would have bought a seat on this ship.
You wouldn't have dated the ocean floor.

There is no downside to this.

Freddy vs Jason VII: Flower Drum Song

I've always been fascinated by the way words
and meanings change over time.

As they travel
with those traveling
to the edge
of all language.

How many times a word
has been used
to mean all different things.

It used to refer to the body.

The body of the earth, the body of a living person.

People's bodies,
plants, animals,
the earth,

Then they came to mean:
The planet.
The sun.
The moon.
The entire solar system.

Then words changed
in what they meant.

And changed the meaning
of the word.

It went from
meaning the thing
that we are made of
to meaning the thing
that our existence depends on.

So, when you say the word earth
you are not quite understanding
what it means.

I.M. Jonathan Livingston Seagull

The first time we came down,
I sat in bed beside a dead bird
and I was really worried.

A whole new language of words
I'd never thought to notice.
I didn't know they were in the house.
One called me "baby."
One called me "father."
One called me "sister."
One called me "mother."

We all shared the same word "mother."
We all shared the same word "water."
We all shared the same, small world.
We all shared,
a broken bird
in our house.

A whole new language of words
I'd never thought to notice.
I didn't know they were in the house.
One called me "baby."
One called me "father."
One called me "sister."
One called me "mother."

We all shared the same word "mother."
We all shared the same word "water."
We all shared the same, small world.

We all shared,
a dead bird
in our house.

A house with a broken house.
A house with a broken bird
in our house.

Jenő's Ghost, The Unfinished Sympathy

I was in my bed,
and I felt like
someone was there.
I closed my eyes
but it was still there
even with my eyes closed.
So I opened my eyes.
It was the sun
coming through my window.
It was the sun that I saw
before I was born.

I was alone on the beach
and everything turned
into a picture.
Everything came together
in my brain and
I could see
everything around me.

The moon, it rose out
of a lake. The waves
moved the moon.
It turned into a cloud
and left my mind.
The clouds left the moon
and the moon left my eyes.

The Endless Exploding Lights

Misery writes poems for breakfast,
then each shovel with fist
flesh to soil, twine rope into pen,
misery severs a spinal cord.
Poetry comes, brings forth its house pet,
stuck crust of scavenger mind,
elephantine great belly.
Words, clumsy as birth, the text
drops wet into an open mouth.
No quick, well chosen, pause,
acrobatic space to cast off,
for poets feasting in unhinged morass,
wetting the mouth without embarrassment,
unscrupulous in food and syrup,
like rats in a maze chewing without restraint
poetic voice gets purged
then meanders back down the corridor,
bleeding towards the molten fountain,
turning around when the elephant roars,
before lumbering back towards the cave.

The Millionaire Fire Fight

Every public house I have lived in,
is now a tear-gas range
for those left against a wall.
Since we moved to the green state
there has not been an apartment free of scorpions
or mice, lurking in corners.
Cheap wine, canned goods
old food for seven hundred years
remains over time on shelf.
Dark secrets, fear.
Poetry, and poetry alone,
should always drink water.
Moonstruck, river gazer, loves those
who are vulnerable, those who are lonely,
poets who look through cracked windows
those who must walk the city or die.
soul spatters into puddles, dries hard,
then joins reflection, next to the skull, to await restoration.
I like writing with you
Because our eyes have not touched,
like the barest breaths of lovers
I cannot know if you know I love you
so, so very much
and who I was and who I'm trying to be
like no-one else, so too, will be no-one else.
Your vision like tincture of night,
fluctuating, striking out, then
you deliver with pointed palm
the rite that emerges from the shaft of gloom.

Wolfpack Beats Per Minute

Words clear nothing
then bleed on
enchantment flows
to myth from vernacular
drones which feed on a destructive
feel it, love, haunt everything
borders, scenery, landscape,
landscape, landscape,
but taste it, taste it
when you breathe in, taste
what have you left behind
the steam from the kettle,
the city on a hill,
those books in the library
I forgot to read for an assignment
that never happened,
what else does this language fail to answer
the horizon of a hidden face
under stalks,
with quiet answers
to questions I should never ask
make me hear you
just between us.

High Tech Madness

I know the moon was blue once
before it stopped being blue.
I know the sky's colour changes.

I don't know where the moon goes
or how the trees are when no one is around
except for a bird or two waiting
to have their nests repaired.

The moon moves in a silent direction,
I watch it go and think about if it was
once blue and where it goes when it
isn't blue anymore. I never saw the sun
or the sky. My mind has pictures of them
so that I can believe in all the things I know.

The Road To Wrestlemania

You go on, I'm not there
I was once but now I'm something
else that I can't name but
it's a thing I have been, a thing
I still am and it never goes away,
my own kind of ghost, my own
kind of death. My death
was never really about death
it was about the end of
being me in the way I was
the way I lived. It was like
a fire, it was like a flood, it was like
a stroke, it was like a war
and it was like an accident
and it was like a fight
and it was like a storm, it was
like a hurricane and it was
like a hurricane and it was
like a hurricane and it was
like a hurricane and it was
like a hurricane and it was
like a hurricane and it

Angry Hipster on Acid

When I woke I was sitting on the church roof at night eating clams, having put cigarettes out on my own eyes while I slept. Somebody below was chipping away at headstones with crooked teeth. I would've filmed it but while I was dying all the lens from my super 8 cameras were stolen by a 6 feet old man made of superglued fingers. It was late but an unknown entity was violently murdering the local Catholic priests, before poisoning egrets with factory farmed petroleum. When I crept back to the hospital, one of the baristas was squabbling with the another. I shouted shit, just pour the drink and move on. I return to the ICU to the raucous sound of canned laughter from 80s sitcoms, but nobody brought a steady procession of Wild Things like I was promised. My ice cream money had been stolen, and a middle-aged woman with the name tag 'Buffy' had followed me back. She reliably informed me that she is the one who causes the entire town, every so often, to wake up at night sweating. I out salt and pepper in the fridge, the pantry, the microwave, and the coffee pot, and set a reminder to go to the supermarket to look for my house key. When I finally fell back into my deathbed, the nurses began updating me every hour, if not more frequently, with what was happening on BBC Two. I watched an allusion to someone called Bill Shakespeare try to stab God, and run to the kitchen. He died of carbon monoxide poisoning. I went to bed, in an old man's sleep, with the feeling I was a show home waiting to be erected. I was never awake, merely dreaming in alliteration.

I Seldom Pray to Rabies

It's hard to walk down the street
when you've got rabies.
I had it when I was a kitten.
I was near some kittens
and some of them bit me,
I got a broken tooth and a bad gash

and some of the blokes I lived with
called me Yoda after Star Wars,
I didn't know what that was,
they just called me Yoda
so I just smiled and stared.

It's like with books
I never read one that got away.
Some people have gone missing
while reading a book.
Some animals never learned to bark.

I can still remember a scene,
that scene is still on my mind
but it's no longer there,
a book now is only a hole in my head,
like a picture torn out of a diary.
I like to think I killed that book,

but that's impossible
because the book is dead.
There was nothing living inside it.
It was a blank book with blank pages.

The very best part of you,
is the part you don't show,
a creature you hate.

Naval

The room is lit by stars.

A dog is barking far.
A cat sits purring by

on my bedside, I hear
noise of traffic in the street.
I smell the rain
outside my house.

There's something I should do,
I feel it's something you should've known

the night before.
In the light of morning
all that had seemed dark,
fading with the morning.
Gathered at my kitchen table
my friend was a new friend
I was glad, I'd never been happy.

We were happy, I was with him, my best friend.
He brought me to my old house,
he took me to my old house,
we drank a pint of whiskey,
he smoked a spliff.

We listened to Bach; and my friend
was talking about his cat.

His cat had been running loose
every night for years.
Now that he's a grown man
it's the first thing he thinks of
when his wife goes out for the day.

Adventures of the Upside-Down Boys

I will tell you about the things I can remember.
The sky always looks very different
when you're flying, it feels like you can reach out
and touch it. I'm lying next to you on the sofa.
The sofa and you are both dirty. The house is a mess.
I wish you were here. There are many things I want to tell you,
but it is hard. I think it would be better if we were sitting
together again, talking in my room. We should have left,

but we didn't know. Do you remember when we went outside
to look for the key? It looked like we were outside forever.
I wanted to go back inside, but there was only you.
Where we came from seemed so much smaller. My father
wanted to talk to my mother but she couldn't understand
what he was saying. It was too loud, then he fell over.
My sister saw me trying to help him but she screamed.
There was blood on the floor. I was too scared to help my father.

I heard the front door slam. I ran out of the house
and was in the park. I started walking. I wanted to look
for someone to save my mother. I wanted to get help
for my father. I wanted to bring my mother back home,
but there was nobody there, just some old buildings.
I saw a train that was about to leave, but it didn't leave.
A long red train, maybe a ferry, but it wasn't moving,
just slowly moving in a circle. I was so cold and scared

and I couldn't move, my legs were heavy. It was hard
to feel my feet. It was so cold, and I couldn't understand
what was going on. I started to cry. I didn't know what to do.

I didn't know what I was supposed to do. I started to shake.
I kept shaking. I remembered being in the park with my mother,
in front of the ice-cream kiosk, before the park. I don't know
why I didn't run away. Maybe I thought the noise was a game.
It was dark outside, but the lights were on inside the kiosk.

I didn't want to go back inside. It was too bright. The smell
of ice cream. I wanted to go to the train station,
but it didn't exist. I started to run. I was running
with all my strength. I heard a man calling my name.
I was running, and it was so dark. It was so dark.
I didn't know where I was running to.

Beethoven's Thirteen Hundredth

I have a friend who cut her finger, and the flesh kept falling off. I have a friend who once shaved a cat in my bathroom and accidentally shaved the bathtub. I have a friend who once dropped a glass of water on a cobra and killed it. I have a friend who caught a water moccasin with his bare hands. I have a friend who ate a live shoe. I had a friend who swallowed a live scorpion. I had a friend who ate a plastic bag full of dirt and grass and she went into convulsions and died. I have a friend who drowned in a puddle of water and tried to find his way out by digging. I have a friend who touched his brother's mouth and he choked to death. I have a friend who drank paint thinner in a bathtub. I have a friend who got on a plane to nowhere to kill some people and then he was killed. I have a friend who tied a big stick to a pig's tail and it hit him in the nose and broke his nose. I have a friend who made a jellyfish sandwich and ate it. I have a friend who was a Navy Seal and he slept with the commandant of his course. I have a friend who hired a male prostitute who dressed in a spider monkey suit to drag him behind a truck. I have a friend who stole a pencil and wrote the word "LOVE" on a wall with it. I have a friend who got two peyote cactuses and ate them. I have a friend who stuffed dry leaves into her body and she went crazy. I have a friend who fell in love with a tree. I have a friend who cut off his own balls and made a necklace out of them. I have a friend who dressed in a bumble bee suit and tried to seduce a train. I have a friend who looked at her blood-drenched hand in the hospital and said, "Well, I guess I'm a murderer." I have a friend who studied the Swiss forest masters to improve her game of pool. I have a friend who mowed lawns for money. I have a friend who walked up to a convenience store and pushed a bag of dog shit through the cashier's window. I have a friend who told his teacher he was in love with the colour purple. I have a friend who sold postage stamps for a living. I have a friend who taught himself to sew and made a dress out of newspaper. I have a friend who sold pot. I have a friend who made a needlepoint of his face. I have a friend who told a doctor she was having sex with her own head. I have a friend who laughed when her boyfriend lost a goldfish in the toilet. I have a friend who sat down on a tiger's tail and stayed there until the tiger ran away. I have a friend who laughed when she cut herself shaving. I have a friend who put a black magic marker in his ear and it burned a hole in his head. I have a friend who chased a clown down a street. I have a friend who drank a whole bottle of Tylenol and swallowed a razor blade. I have a friend who went to the dentist for a cleaning and was shocked when he saw a baby tooth. I have a friend who ate a glass of water and fainted. I have a friend who threw a penny at a lightning bolt. I have a friend who swallowed a tree branch and broke his neck. I have a friend who swallowed a dead body. I have a friend who inhaled a balloon and passed out. I have a friend who urinated on an electric fence and got shot with a stun gun. I have a friend who ate a bottle of cologne. I have a friend who stuffed newspaper into his ears and then he got a headache. I have a friend who burned his nose and spat blood on a clown. I have a friend who wrote a brief article about himself in the newspaper. I have a friend who owned and managed a successful record store for 20 years. I have a friend who ran a newspaper. I have a friend who wrote a very good book. I have a friend who founded a small company. I have a friend who was stabbed in the neck with an ice pick. I have a friend who banged his head against a brick wall and was in a coma for two days. I have a friend who killed himself with a stapler. I have a friend who put toothpaste in his anus. I have a friend who performed oral sex on a banana. I have a friend who sewed his wife's hair to the waistband of his shorts. I have a friend who mixed his urine with alcohol and drank it. I have a friend who threw a pie at the Pope. I have a friend who set himself on fire in a mall. I have a friend who shit on the top of a moving train. I have a friend who put needles in his eye and didn't notice. I have a friend who used a shoehorn to put her head through a wall. I have a friend who put his head inside a grenade. I have a friend who chewed glass and his mouth and nose were sewn shut. I have a friend who put perfume in his ears and slept with one ear open. I have a friend who pinched his own nipples until they bled. I have a friend who wrote a bad review of the Toronto Symphony Orchestra. I have a friend who gave himself a bath and kept his finger in the water the whole time. I have a friend who bled to death from a paper cut. I have a friend who cut her tongue in half. I have a friend who bought $1.50 worth of gum and put $2.00 worth in her pocket. I have a friend who tried to eat his own hair. I have a friend who tied a knot in his shoelace and got blood poisoning. I have a friend who coughed up a lung. I have a friend who drowned in a fishbowl. I have a friend who sat in a bucket of fish. I have a friend who threw a jar of jam in a river. I have a friend who was swallowed by a whale. I have a friend who froze himself to death in a snowstorm. I have a friend who came out of the ocean with his skin on fire. I have a friend who shot a can off a roof to see if it would fly. I have a friend who had sex with a ghost. I have a friend who set himself on fire to see if he could feel it burn. I have a friend who set his car on fire and tried to crawl through the burning wreckage to safety. I have a friend who ate a cyanide capsule and survived. I have a friend who wanted to be an actor but got stuck in traffic. I have a friend who ate a package of nuts and was only served a second helping. I have a friend who climbed a fountain and drank the water. I have a friend who cut his ear off with a lawnmower and woke up the next day. I have a friend who dug his own grave and suffocated himself in it. I have a friend who built a catapult and wanted to know what it was like to be hit in the testicles by a shot from that catapult. I have a friend who ate a live moth and woke up two days later in a field of yellow daisies. I have a friend who took a pill and threw up in front of a mirror and got a great idea for a new sales strategy. I have a friend who shaved his face and chest in the same sitting. I have a friend who kicked a tree stump and made it explode. I have a friend who put a lit cigarette in her ear and blew it out with a shotgun. I have all these friends and not a single story to tell.

If You Think There is Too Much Scent

Taken one step at a time,
so the earth can breathe a little slower too.
But we are all creatures of light and dark.
We know what kind of life
a pine tree can withstand.
This isn't poetry about dead whales,
or polar bears. There is nothing poetic at all
about any animal's being dead for a reason
that has nothing to do with my garden,

The purpose of the Forest of Dead Wood Art Project
is to create the most copies of The Dead Wood Art Project.

A forest is my forest —
my forest of a lifetime —
so no one is going to come
and remove all the trees
in my forest or my forest of life.
I'm sorry you must die.
But you're dead and gone.

We can't stop the process,
but the world, including the forest,
does turn over each second —
it is not a fixed place.

Take Out a Gun and Blow off your Foot

I grabbed onto the neck of
a loose dog that had bitten me
once. It didn't seem dangerous,

just a pain in the back of my knee
and a joy at the shock of the
bite, but the owner was furious.

He took me and bit my hand
as if there were little coins
in his mouth.

Secret texts of a Horror Story

Not being ever found.
          An ocean without a song,
                    as sirens laughing
                              as people sacrificed.

Blank, entire field of night.

A cloak where there's light,
          not of joy, of meditation
                    free-style
                              My shapeless self

Spills unarticulated life,

for awhile in crystal,
          fastest on the silent
                    planet, in blind spot
                              of phone, radio,

soil, granite,

toppings, of seas
          Deepest human not having anything there,
                    in bathroom, in trees. A calm place
                              in a snowed-over city, where

snow pelts, a squirrel sleeps in front

of a window
        under roof, poufed
                and ragged, gray,
                        but no footprints in snow.

Cocksaw.

I like the idea of this poem.
        Let it be yours.
                smoke snow-ice.
                        Healing powers of slow-dawn

overbruised skies snowflakes,

colors distant that's
        my skin. Nothing strange,
                no stranger than I but snow
                        with sinuses makes me weep.

There All Right

There's a ghost that's running along the ceiling.
(Take one at random and it's already in the wall)
You've seen this ghost before.
Hate him, love him.
Now he's free.
You've got to remember this.
He is everywhere.
His fingers are clumsily waving over here
(and then it's in your face)
and I'm bleeding (bleeding)
as he leaves me
(and finally)
his name is Hate.
(I just died)
with my hands bleeding.
I'm dead (died)
and there's nothing I can do about it
(I died)
I've seen The Ghost of Hate (killed me)
from the beginning
(death)
the beginning (I died)
What are you gonna do with this life (rotten)
(half-dead) (won't die) (hates me) (dead)?
Ghost (home of the soldiers)
everything about you (both sides)
everything about you (both sides)
everything about you (both sides)
everything about you (both sides)
everything about you (both sides)

This One's Tiny Friend

My headless body was hanging in the tree.
I couldn't tell if it was a ghost
or a figment of my imagination.
I ran to the grocery store to get an axe.
I thought I could kill the tree.

I came back with a car. The tree fell.
I put my head on a spoon
and ate it by candlelight
and threw up, poisonous.

I put my head on a
B-52 bomber.
I left it in a phone booth
in Dallas, Texas.
There are flying saucers hovering
in the sky, and my head
is on a table at Sydney Opera House.

I'm on the roof.
My head is at sea.

Strong and Tall and Missing

It's not that I want to
give you any comfort
that this was so easily
taken away.
It's not that I want to
betray the empathy that you
shared with me
and the empathy
that it's safe to assume
you're feeling right now.
But I can't deny it
and I can't explain it
and I can't ignore
that you did
tireless work to find me
and that you found me
without putting me through
a gauntlet of tortures
and let's face it
without really giving me much
to believe in.
It's that after
an entire life dedicated
to loving someone,
at least partially
they are done
trying to keep the peace
for their own comfort
and not for mine
and that I can't

keep my breath
to myself.
Please don't call.
I'll be here
pining for you to see
the cold that's now
brewing in my chest
at the sound of your
cold voice.

Out Back to Worth into the Mind

The air was like a million
and you stood there feeling sick.
You turned and looked down at your
jeans that were all torn apart
from the waist down.

I am a poet and this
Is my work of art.

Your body loved you so you
kissed it all over. You thought
what's a poet for? To make you
and your body feel nothing that
would hurt you as you walk out
from all of us.

That's when I saw the broken
mirror in the house. No one cleaned
it out, and I can feel something coming.
Oh I can't see so much, but I can hear.
There's a pain I can hear and feel
at the same time. I put my hand
inside yours and that's when
you said I must be
a very sad man.

I've been here in this room
bitter from the heart sick soul;
lonely and alone.

I held my ears open, you poured in
your tears — O, such painful hearses.
I can help you with the cabinets
when they start rattling like a ship from
the side of the street going up a hill

Then what you feel I feel all over.

The Last Night was the Last Night not the First

If someone starts screaming,
we might find an ear on the floor.
If they aren't screaming
they probably have the same
dream every time. You can hear
the ocean when there's no electricity.
It's hard to hear it under
all that screaming. It is dark
and you're there under the screaming.
We are all afraid it might happen again.
I wish the ocean was louder. We could
see what it really looks like
if the ocean was yelling louder.
We might just find an ear
on a shelf in an ear museum.
The ear on the end of "the thing"
comes out when you find the thing.
One last ear will keep the thing quiet.

The thing looks so real
that it won't be easy to see it.
It might be one of your grandfathers.
It might be a fish. At least it is
something. But it is made of nothing,
except for that thing. It might be
some kind of boat made
with the most valuable thing.
The boat might not smell right.
You don't usually know
what an ocean smells like

and the ocean doesn't usually feel
like the ocean unless there are waves
on the water. I once saw an eye, it was blue
and I tried it with some sugar water
and I thought it would help but it seemed
to have a mind of its own. It didn't work.
It tried to eat the finger I stabbed
its eye with on an island.

Tried to Remember the Party

If everything is nothing,
just a nothing,
the universe and her heart,
the stars a mirror,
and we can do whatever
as you're standing beside me
all the way. We're going
to the edge and we'll go again.

It might not be your time but
it will be when it wants to be.

Just when it wants to be.

One morning everything will
fall into the empty room of your head;
You will still have your face
as if on a card that you've
sketched it upon.

How will I know if I'm alone
When I'm never alone?

I hope a tree will hold a piece
of you, to fall at night,
to see the moon.

Sometimes a song will come
like a dream that comes like
a song. When all is left is ash
I will go.

watch someone starve) lost bravas
from passports vomit less not remind
themselves about trying again letting
bands blast telly has suppressed traces

of sparks (didn't report garden bomb
to Interpol as vital being
no one sleeps with their head
between their knees

except in the arms
of a mother,
a friend,
or a lover

those who got mummified to be left alone

he's a man who thinks of time as if
to me the trees are of this century.
The one thing you do when you're young
is to think of time.

In my house the cat sits for hours
the same cat who's in the family for ages,
            or at least the same as

in his eyes he found what he was looking for:
a woman with a face like that of a mannequin.

(Let others tell the paradox).

he takes in more or less of the same
all you've been doing this whole while

what it doesn't look like is
the fact that he is on no account to know
    if it is

the trees are of this century.
            and they say
            that the sun goes up into my heart
when all of you do,

The sun doesn't rise up inside you.
Your heart goes up.
the sun doesn't go down in you
and that if you should

If you should

If we're going to see such things
there's a price to pay.

The summer was huge, and hugely gone.
   what happens when
            (i.e., we have the sun
                  in our souls
)

a kind of god it will ever be
that's how the world's made to be
but the trees are of this century
for

a kind of god.

Like Red Screaming from Home

My brothers and I lived in a house
that had been knocked about a bit
and still smelled of the sea, I remember
in our basement the sound of an iron
being dragged across the floor.

The first place you remember — when
I was a boy — for it to be over, when I
could get to the end of the porch and breathe
in. We are the only thing that will never
be over, but I'll let you down now.

> *I believe in everything*
> *that the world stands for…*
> *the idea that anything*
> *at all is not in itself absurd,*
> *and that anything I never wanted*
> *to tell, as I'd never have a reason*
> *to tell it. Everything at once.*

My Angry Days

And each one of us have said
our dead are with us and have not died.
They are merely back in the dawn
with sadness, but if you wait,
a little fire extinguishes it.

Just like the things that go, the furniture
is on fire, some nights blizzarded
by hand, time, milk, us gathering
on a leash screaming *flatlines*
and *cigars* from the windows.

Three Starving

Show me the road, I said, *any road*. Teach me
a stupid song that wakes me up before
I sleep, and if, one day, you may want
to know how I find myself in the dark
without needing a compass. i know
where I've been. To love is for the living
but the sunshine is sick and I cannot stop it.

 I feel so lost for you are my home,
and therefore we are strangers.
A bit more coffee from the robin
today; I can just about taste it.
We're going with oxygen this weekend.

I have deodorant in my ears
and the mirror wants to touch up its front teeth.
We're going to lie here in the dark
and a beautiful butterfly is going to land
on my mouth. That is how I will know
to expect a quiet night. The same silent burn.

Last Year is Swimming in a Cup of Blood

We'll all float into the distance,
this could be a full moon after all:
fragile, glacially beautiful.
The poor guy, mining its cheeses
to pay off an old debt. We've noticed
what was left of him and you said
there's something wrong with that sort
of thing, and then you began to laugh.'

If you're feeling hard-done-by
interpret these whispers: the TV
may be too big, the blood coffee thicker
than it should be, no off-duty moon
cops to place a pulse on an EKG,
just a robot that sings their blues.

The one-eyed man isn't gone,
he watches you stare out the window
though there is nothing in sight
but the end of that street and his
remaining eye – the eye that is turning,
the eye that is slowly taking on
the shade of a poet who remains absent.

There's only you and there's only
that sightless man, and we're both
going to die one day.

I'm Honestly Only Writing Because I'm Scared of what Happens when I Don't

the difference between being a dog
of a song that keeps my body awake
as the ocean laps and the beaches
sink into your bed to wake up
ive been thinking about the night
when i first opened my ears
when the first
i would die and you
my bones will fall with no trace ill leave no trace
my father once said
when we were lying
we could have saved it
a long distance my heart is always
and the next one
cant wait on any better deal
the second you walk into
the second you come home drunk
we could have used it for lunch
in a time capsule
is the best
and you said we can
the time capsule
is where well come out i guess
i think about having an oblong grave
i think about when i was a child in a dream
the sky would just open in
not one person in the whole wide world
in the rain
my body when broken

its been a real privilege
you mean i wasnt there
the next one will take my seat
the second you walk into my bed
when the sky opened up a bit of snow
like a song on your mouth
you should be able to sing
when the heart stops beating
when the sky opens up
its never easy
the second that this is over
is never enough
the clouds are still
they seem to me this morning
like the skin
and my hands all blue
when everything changes its just that
if im gonna be up all night
its fine by me
its going down
you have a new skin
but the ocean in the room
doesnt go away
were having a celebration
my house is burning it was
is like nothing to do with my life
there will be time enough to lie about why
thats not a bird
when things get very dark
im going to tell you a secret?
the first thing this one sees?
a white picket fence
and then the other one sees a light
my heart is going like a drum

it wont stop playing
i dont think i know myself
in its own way
i was like
im in hell
the sun still shines
just when it gets dark at my house
the song the old man sings
but the world is ending
and someone wants something else
you know what this is
this is the feeling we have
when somethings not right with this
and it doesnt matter
ive been looking for
well go back to bed i guess
the way i see the stars above the bed
will keep us warm you think
well just sleep it off tonight
the first thing is that the sun
when nothing is not right with this
when things dont quite go
the next one cant wait
on better deals
for a moment like this
i just get this
its too late
were both going out tonight
my hand can barely
ill wait for you
after my head hits the pillow
because i dont think
i know that you dont
dont know why i know that

i dont know why i know
it might be that thing again
i was at a concert the night we were
when you were just leaving
there was somebody i wanted
something inside that i couldnt
that never should have been
left out
you just came home tonight
im getting more and more nervous
its time for another
i might do some harm with it
i think about the first
i wish that i wasnt this way
cause you have no choice
you have to learn whats true and whats wrong
you are like a child and a mother
there in your mothers house again
in some way
i need to go outside right now
and try this some more
i think about you
what you had on your mind
was always this far away
we should be able to do
whatever you want to do
you can make all the right decisions
about your own time
but i cant make it stop
that when the time comes
it will all be very clean
with no trace and nothing left
we might be all alone
when this is done

i hope you can understand
when i leave it all here with you
i am in love with all of this
the next thing this one looks at
is not this person at all
the heart stops beating
it will not be very nice of it
im never going to be with my friends
because one day they all will die
so do they matter to you
the last thing you see is
my heart stops beating
and i dont think that
there is anyway to live
the next one looks at the moon
you dont want to see what i see
in your eyes or your eyes
when the blood
is going out
of some of my best friends
when the ocean licks a beach
it never goes away
the waves go down in the tide
and the heart beats
when i was younger i didnt like the world
i only liked a lot of people
if you dont remember who
itll be all right with them
when they all came to their senses
when the time passes
and then you know
what to think about
when you think about whats true
and then i think about what you said

when we were having it
if you dont remember me at all
you know that the best thing i can do
is go on living
and i remember the way that it was
i got more than the last one
got it all so i just won
so i just cant wait
i should go now
when i was younger i liked a lot
of the wrong people
when you said something else
when the day is over and everything is said
my body will go away
and the next one cant wait
on a better deal
you are like a child
in your mothers house again
in some way
i know there must be a reason
that i cannot see it all the way down
the world is ending and
i wish i wasnt this way
because you have no choice
i love you too
and that this would disappear
my heart has just stopped

and the sound of voices nearby

All I want
is to walk
in the palm-
lined hollow.
I no longer
sleep at night,
the problems
I could see
I cannot, and
that's all I have
to say. (There
is nothing
after this.)

We're One Shot

Waiting For the Light/Battle In The Skies

Barbed wire, in the drowsy surf,
makes a pattern like a mirror.
You can call me tomorrow
and I'll explain a light camera,
a code to be master,
a projector with my name on it,
and a sign of the grave.
So, will you come to my farewell
party? I'll come if you do.
I thought I heard myself fall
down the stairs a lot last night.

Acknowledgements

I have been blessed to find new friends in the UK and throughout the world who have shared their experiences with me and to discover a new community. For any omissions, errors or for any comments, corrections, questions, criticisms, suggestions of additions or requests for information, comments, clarifications, I wish to remain, as always, open-minded and willing to learn more and help contribute.

I would like to acknowledge persons who are important in many aspects of my life; my brothers, for being the people who made me realise that I could become 'whatever I put my mind to'. And my partner for the many hours spent discussing and debating books, ideas, and history. Their encouragement, support, and willingness is deeply appreciated.

Forget a single book, for it is the collective power of the whole that, far from being too much for us, is often enough to make us believe, though it is no small thing, that we are what we can imagine ourselves to be.

When one has lived long enough, one understands the concept of living for the sake of life as it unfolds in a life. For many, for many of us life is a struggle between what it can be and what it must be. In the process, it is a struggle between what we know or suspect and that which we can't know. The key is to be better.

All human beings have tendencies that are destructive and all can strive to be good. This is a struggle with the limits of human nature. It has often been said that you will not meet anyone who doesn't lie and you will not meet anyone who hasn't been cruel to someone else. This is the truth of humanity. We struggle against the limits, the constraints that we experience in everyday life.

LAYO

UTYO

URUN

REST

CPSIA information can be obtained
at www.ICGtesting.com
Printed in the USA
LVHW110814240722
724256LV00004B/217